Dear Parent:

Congratulations! Your child is taking the first steps on an exciting journey. The destination? Independent reading!

STEP INTO READING® will help your child get there. The program offers five steps to reading success. Each step includes fun stories and colorful art. There are also Step into Reading Sticker Books, Step into Reading Math Readers, Step into Reading Phonics Readers, Step into Reading Write-In Readers, and Step into Reading Phonics Boxed Sets—a complete literacy program with something to interest every child.

Learning to Read, Step by Step!

Ready to Read   Preschool–Kindergarten
• big type and easy words • rhyme and rhythm • picture clues
For children who know the alphabet and are eager to begin reading.

Reading with Help   Preschool–Grade 1
• basic vocabulary • short sentences • simple stories
For children who recognize familiar words and sound out new words with help.

Reading on Your Own   Grades 1–3
• engaging characters • easy-to-follow plots • popular topics
For children who are ready to read on their own.

Reading Paragraphs   Grades 2–3
• challenging vocabulary • short paragraphs • exciting stories
For newly independent readers who read simple sentences with confidence.

Ready for Chapters   Grades 2–4
• chapters • longer paragraphs • full-color art
For children who want to take the plunge into chapter books but still like colorful pictures.

STEP INTO READING® is designed to give every child a successful reading experience. The grade levels are only guides. Children can progress through the steps at their own speed, developing confidence in their reading, no matter what their grade.

Remember, a lifetime love of reading starts with a single step!

Step into Reading, Random House, and the Random House colophon are registered trademarks of Random House, Inc.

Visit us on the Web!
StepIntoReading.com
randomhouse.com/kids
Seussville.com

Educators and librarians, for a variety of teaching tools, visit us at randomhouse.com/teachers

Library of Congress Cataloging-in-Publication Data
Rabe, Tish.
Look for the Lorax / by Tish Rabe ; illustrated by Christopher Moroney and Jan Gerardi.
   p. cm. — (Step into reading. Step 1)
Summary: Easy-to-read, rhyming text introduces the Lorax and the place he calls home.
ISBN 978-0-375-86999-0 (trade) — ISBN 978-0-375-96999-7 (lib. bdg.)
[1. Stories in rhyme. 2. Imaginary creatures—Fiction.] I. Moroney, Christopher; Gerardi, Jan, ill.
II. Seuss, Dr. Lorax. III. Title.
PZ8.3.R1145 Loo 2012 [E]—dc22 2010050820

Printed in the United States of America
10 9 8 7 6 5 4 3 2 1

Look for the LORAX

by Tish Rabe

illustrated by Christopher Moroney
and Jan Gerardi

Random House New York

Blue sky.
Clouds fly.
Bright trees sway.

Cute suits!
Bar-ba-loots
play, play, play.

Bump, jump.

Jump, bump.

Run,

run,

run.

Hop, hop.

Flip, flop.

Fun,

fun,

fun.

11

The Lorax sees swans
swim, swim, swim.

The Lorax hears swans
sing to him.

Fruit sweet
to eat.
Yum, yum, yum.

Humming-Fish.

Happy fish.

Hum, hum, hum.

Big fish.

Little fish.

Swish, swish, swish.

High fish.

Low fish.

Splish, splash, splish!

The Lorax sees birds
fly on by.

Fast bird.

Slow bird.

Fly, fly, fly.

Bright day.

Light day.

Sky is clear.

The Lorax says, "I'll stay . . ."

"... right here."